Grape Season

By Sunita Apte
Illustrated by Tim Jones

Scott Foresman
is an imprint of

Glenview, Illinois • Boston, Massachusetts • Chandler, Arizona •
Upper Saddle River, New Jersey

Illustrations
Timothy Jones.

Photographs

Every effort has been made to secure permission and provide appropriate credit for photographic material. The publisher deeply regrets any omission and pledges to correct errors called to its attention in subsequent editions.

Unless otherwise acknowledged, all photographs are the property of Pearson Education, Inc.

21 Photodisc/Alamy.

ISBN 13: 978-0-328-51385-7
ISBN 10:   0-328-51385-7

12 13 V0FL 17 16 15

Miguel stood up. He was tired from pulling weeds out of Tía Julia's vegetable garden. His knees ached. He wished he could be out in the grape fields with his sister and father, helping to earn money for the family. Instead, Miguel was at Tía Julia's with the other kids who were too young to pick grapes. Their job was to complete the chores.

Early August was grape season in California's central valley. The heat blazed, and Miguel's mother, father, and sister had to work hard picking the grape crop in the fields. They sorted the grapes and put them on big trays in the sun to dry into raisins.

Miguel thought about the kids in his class who got to take vacations in the summer, going to the beach or the mountains. He thought about lazy summer days, waking up and reading, and drinking lemonade in the cool shade.

Miguel's summer certainly wasn't like that. He had worked hard for Tía Julia since school got out at the beginning of June. In fact, Miguel had worked hard in Tía Julia's garden every summer since he started going to school. Miguel's family was just a few of the thousands of migrant workers hired every summer to pick grapes, but he was too young to go with them.

Going back to school in late August would be a relief for Miguel. He looked forward to his classes in the large, cool school building. Nights would be spent doing homework, not falling into bed so tired he could barely think.

He envied his sister, Luisa, who got to go out to the fields. Instead of helping the family like his sister, Miguel had to stay behind with all the other kids who were too young to work in the fields.

"I can't wait until I'm old enough to pick,"
Miguel would say almost every night. "I'll fill
500 trays a day. Just wait and see."

Sometimes Luisa would argue with him.
"Picking grapes is not fun at all," she would
say. "The hot sun blazes down and makes the
sweat run into your eyes and sting. The water
in your canteen gets so warm by the end of the
day, you can't even drink it! And besides, you
wouldn't be able to fill 500 trays in one day.
I can only fill 250 trays a day, and even Papa
can only fill 400."

Their papa thought Miguel was funny. "You
will have plenty of time to pick grapes, *mi hijo*,"
he would say. "Enjoy your freedom now, son."

Miguel smiled as he finished his work at Tía Julia's for the day. Today was special. His Tío Hector was coming down from Fresno that evening to visit. Hector was his favorite uncle. He always brought a gift for him and talked to him like he was a grown-up. Luisa loved him too.

Mama had left the fields early since Tío Hector was coming. She was making fresh tortillas when Miguel got back to the cabin. Tío Hector was already there, talking to Mama and sneaking bites of chicken. Mama made a big show of shooing him away, but Miguel could tell she didn't really mind. Mama loved Hector too. Everyone did.

Tío Hector was a clown, always making jokes. He laughed with the family all through dinner. Then, as Mama was serving dessert, he cleared his throat. Miguel could tell he wanted to say something important.

"Santiago," Hector said as he turned toward Miguel's father. "I'm planning to go camping in Sequoia National Park this weekend. I was wondering if I could take Luisa and Miguel with me. They've never been there, and it would be a nice vacation for them."

Miguel and Luisa couldn't believe their ears. They waited breathlessly for Papa's answer. But Papa shook his head. "No. It's not possible. Luisa must work in the fields this weekend, and Miguel must help Tía Julia."

Miguel and Luisa exchanged a glance. Miguel could see the tears beginning to form in Luisa's eyes. Then they both looked at the floor. Papa was such a mule. They knew they couldn't change his mind. He worked too hard and needed their help at home and in the fields. But Miguel would do anything for the chance to go on a real vacation.

Tío Hector put his hand on Papa's arm. "But it's summer, Santiago. And they're kids. They need a break. It would be a great experience for them."

"I heard Sequoia National Park is beautiful," Mama chimed in softly. "Luisa works hard in the fields," she added.

"And I work hard in Tía Julia's garden," Miguel added.

"I know you do mi hijo," said Mama as she looked imploringly at Papa.

Papa stared at the pleading faces of his family surrounding him. "Okay, okay, they can go. I guess we can do without Luisa for the weekend. And Julia will find a way to manage, as well."

"Oh, thank you, Papa!" Miguel said as he jumped up and threw his arms around his father. Then Miguel hugged Tío Hector. This was the best present Tío Hector had ever brought.

Miguel couldn't believe that he was going on a vacation just like other kids did during the summer. He thought about how he would casually mention his trip when school began again. The rich kids always bragged about what they had done during the summer. He and the other pickers' children always kept quiet.

Now, when the subject came up, he wouldn't need to keep quiet. He could honestly say, "Oh, I went camping in Sequoia National Park with my uncle."

There was bright sunshine and a clear blue sky on the day of the camping trip. Miguel and Luisa got up extra early and helped their mother clean the cabin. Papa had already gone to the fields. Miguel ran up the road to check for Tío Hector's car every five minutes.

Finally, Tío Hector arrived. The trunk of his car was loaded with a tent, food, and other gear. Luisa and Miguel added their sleeping bags and backpacks to the rest of the supplies. Excited to go, they hugged Mama goodbye and hopped in the car.

"Let's hit the road!" Miguel cried.

Tío Hector started the engine and drove away. Miguel looked back and saw his mother standing in the doorway of the cabin. Mama's face was beaming, and she was grinning from ear to ear. *Mama is so happy we're getting a chance to go on this vacation,* Miguel thought. *I wish she and Papa could have come with us. They need a vacation too.*

Sequoia National Park was about two hours away. For the first hour or so, they drove through dry, flat farmland. Tío Hector's car passed acres of almond and orange trees. Then, suddenly, hills loomed in the distance. Tío Hector pointed to them.

"See those hills?" he asked the kids. "Those are the foothills of the Sierra Nevada. The park is in those mountains. That's where the sequoias, the giant trees, are. We'll drive into those hills and keep going up until we're above 6,000 feet. Our campground is at an elevation of 6,700 feet.

Soon, the road started to twist and turn. They reached the park gate, and Tío Hector paid the fee. Then they drove on. Miguel stared out the window. It was hard to believe this beautiful place was only two hours from where they lived. He wondered why he had never heard about this place.

Tío Hector saw the look on his nephew's face. "It's amazing, isn't it?" he said softly. "When you're at Tía Julia's, it's almost impossible to think a place like this exists."

Thirty minutes later, they reached their campsite at Lodgepole. Luisa and Miguel helped Tío Hector set up the tent. Once it was up, they put their sleeping bags and backpacks inside the tent. Then they put all their food in a metal storage box.

"That's to keep the food safe from bears," Tío Hector explained. "The bears in Sequoia are accustomed to humans. They might come to the campsite looking for our food if we leave it out."

Luisa and Miguel exchanged glances. *Would we see a bear on one of our hikes?* Miguel wondered. *How cool!* Luisa was not as excited. "They won't try to come into our tent, will they, Tío Hector?" she pleaded.

"No," said Tío Hector. "They are only interested in our food. We'll be fine as long as we use that metal box."

Once the campsite was set up, they drove to the trailhead of their first hike. They were going to see the General Sherman Tree, the world's largest tree. They hiked down the trail past other huge sequoias until they reached the General Sherman. Miguel's eyes widened when he saw it. He didn't know trees could be so big.

"Wow," Miguel said. "You could fit ten of me inside its trunk!"

"Yes," said Tío Hector. "This tree is about 275 feet tall, and the trunk is about 103 feet around."

"How long does it take to grow so big?" Miguel wondered.

"How long do you think?" Tío Hector asked. "One hundred years?" Miguel guessed.

Tío Hector smiled. "Not quite so fast. This tree is more than 2,300 years old. Even though they grow fast, it takes a long time to get this big."

Tío Hector took a picture of Luisa and Miguel standing in front of the tree. They felt like ants standing next to the General Sherman. *I can't wait to show Mama and Papa this picture when we go home,* Miguel thought as they walked back to the car.

They still had one more trail they wanted to hike that day—the trail to the top of Moro Rock. As they pulled into the lot by the Moro Rock trailhead, Miguel saw something moving around by the picnic tables.

"Look, a bear!" he cried.

Sure enough, a small bear was ambling through the picnic site. It had knocked over trashcans, and it was snooping around picnic tables. It was scouring the entire picnic site searching for any leftover scraps of food. The three watched the bear from the safety of the car until it disappeared into the trees.

"Wow!" was all Miguel could say. "Wow!"

The hike up Moro Rock was harder than the General Sherman hike. Luisa huffed and puffed as she trudged up the side of the rocky outcropping. It was worth it, though. The view from Moro Rock was spectacular. Around them were high mountain peaks, and below stretched valley after valley.

"I thought this would be a good hike for the first day," Tío Hector told them. "The view here gives you a good sense of the park." He pointed to their left at a distant meadow surrounded by snowcapped peaks. "Tomorrow, if the weather is nice, we'll hike over there."

That night, back at the camp, Miguel climbed into his sleeping bag after dinner. Around him, he could hear the sounds of the forest. Tomorrow they would take more hikes, including one to Crescent Meadow. On the way, they might get to drive through the trunk of a fallen sequoia. Imagine a tree big enough to drive through!

Miguel sleepily imagined Mama and Papa back in the cabin, after a hard day of picking grapes. It was funny how being somewhere else made you see things differently. Before this trip, plants and trees were just part of his chores, things that made him miserable. Now he could see that they were also things of great beauty. Things that could give people joy. He loved being outside in nature. Thanks to Tío Hector, he learned that nature brought more to life than just work.

Miguel closed his eyes and drifted off to sleep thinking, *Next summer I'll find a way to bring Mama and Papa here. They deserve time to enjoy nature too.*

California's Central Valley

California's Central Valley stretches almost 400 miles, from Bakersfield in the south to Redding in the north. Mountains rise on both sides of the valley. To the west are the Coastal Ranges, and to the east are the Sierra Nevada.

The Central Valley is known for its agriculture, or the growing of food. It is often referred to as the "fruit basket of the world." About one-fourth of all the fruits and vegetables Americans eat are produced in the Central Valley. Crops include grapes, oranges, and almonds.

These crops need people to plant and pick them. That job usually falls to migrant, or seasonal, workers. These workers travel around the Central Valley, following the harvest of each crop.

Redding

Fresno

Bakersfield

Sacramento

Sequoia National Park